FastTrack MUSIC INSTRUCTION

Lead Singer For

INTRODUCTION

Welcome back to FastTrack®!

Hope you enjoyed *Lead Singer 1* and are ready to sing some hits. Have you and your friends formed a band? Or do you feel like soloing with the CD? Either way, make sure you're relaxed and your voice is warmed-up…it's time to sing!

With the knowledge you already have from *Lead Singer 1*, you're ready to sing all eight of these great songs. But it's still important to remember the three Ps: **patience, practice,** and **pace yourself.**

As with *Lead Singer 1*, don't try to bite off more than you can chew. If your voice tires, take some time off. If you get frustrated, put down the music and just listen to the CD. If you forget something, go back to the method book and learn it. If you're doing fine, think about booking a gig at a local venue!

CONTENTS

CD Track	Song Title	Page
1	Blue Suede Shoes	4
2	Dreams	6
3	I Just Called to Say I Love You	9
4	Let It Be	13
5	(You Make Me Feel Like) A Natural Woman	16
6	Piece of My Heart	19
7	Surfin' U.S.A.	24
8	Wonderful Tonight	27

ABOUT THE CD

Again, you get a CD with the book! Each song in the book is included on the CD, so you can hear how it sounds and sing along when you're ready.

Each example on the CD is preceded by one measure of "clicks" to indicate the tempo and meter. Pan right to hear the vocal part emphasized. Pan left to hear the accompaniment (the band) emphasized.

HAL•LEONARD® CORPORATION

7777 W. BLUEMOUND RD. P.O. BOX 13819 MILWAUKEE, WI 53213

Copyright © 2000 by HAL LEONARD CORPORATION
International Copyright Secured   All Rights Reserved

Visit Hal Leonard Online at
www.halleonard.com

LEARN SOMETHING NEW EACH DAY

We know you're eager to start singing these great songs, but first we should alert you to a couple of new things. We'll make it brief—only two pages...

Keys

We haven't used any new key signatures here. They're all familiar to you from *Lead Singer 1*. However, don't forget about them! Make sure you know which sharps (or flats) to use before singing each song:

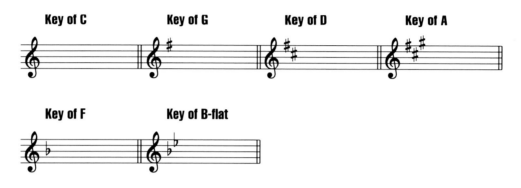

Ranges

Just to keep things interesting, we've used a male and a female singer. But don't think you can't sing every single song...regardless of your gender. If it's in your range, then go for it!

What Is That Little Symbol?

That little dot/moon over the rest at the end of several songs is called a **fermata**.

It simply means to "hold" an unspecified amount of time. That is to say that the.tempo will not be the same during a fermata. You can hold the note (or rest) as long as you like. (Of course, we didn't want to keep paying the band, so we just cut them off after a few beats.)

Song Structure

Most songs have different sections, which might be recognizable by any or all of the following markers above the top staff.

1 INTRODUCTION (or "Intro"): This is a short section at the beginning that (you guessed it again!) "introduces" the song to the listeners.

2 VERSES: One of the main sections of the song is the **verse**. There will usually be several verses, all with the same music but each with different lyrics.

3 CHORUS: Perhaps the most memorable section of a song is the **chorus**. Again, there might be several choruses, but each chorus will often have the same lyrics and music.

4 BRIDGE: This section makes a transition from one part of a song to the next. For example, you may find a **bridge** between the chorus and next verse.

5 SOLOS: Sometimes **solos** are played over the verse or chorus structure, but in some songs the solo section has its own structure. During a solo, the singer has a few choices: dance, run around on stage, sit and clean your toes… your choice!

6 OUTRO: Similar to the "intro," this section brings the song to an end.

That's about it! Enjoy the music…

Blue Suede Shoes

Words and Music by Carl Lee Perkins

Verse
Fast Rock 'n' Roll ♩ = 190

1. Well, it's one for the mon-ey, two for the show, three to get read-y now

Chorus

go, cat, go, but don't __ you __ step on my blue suede shoes.

Well, you can do an-y-thing __ but lay off __ of my blue suede shoes.

Verse

2. Well, you can knock me down, __ step in my face, __ slan-der my name all

o-ver the place. __ Well, do an-y-thing __ that you wan-na do, __ but, uh-uh, hon-ey, lay off __

Chorus

__ of them shoes, and don't __ you step on my blue suede shoes.

Well, you can do an-y-thing __ but lay off __ of my blue suede shoes. Let's go

Guitar Solo

cats!

3. Well, you can

Verse

burn my house, __ steal my car, __ drink my li-quor from an old fruit jar. Well,

Dreams

Words and Music by Stevie Nicks

Intro

Moderately ♩ = 120

Verse

1. Now here you go ___ a - gain. ___ You say ___ you want ___ your free -

- dom. Well, who am I ___ to keep ___ you down? ___

It's on - ly right ___

___ that you ___ should play the way ___ you feel ___ it. But

lis - ten care - ful - ly ___ to the sound ___ of your lone -

- li - ness, like a heart - beat, drives you mad, ___ in the still -

- ness of re - mem - ber - ing ___ what you had ___

and what you lost ___ and what you had ___

___ and what you lost. ___

Chorus

Oh, thun - der on - ly hap - pens when it's rain -

- ing. Play - ers on - ly love

____ you when they're play - ing. ____ Say,

wom - en, they will come ___ and they will go. ____

When the rain ___ wash - es ____ you clean, you'll know. _

Guitar Solo

You'll know. ____

Verse

2. Now, here I go ___ a - gain ___ I see cry - stal ____ vi - sions.

I keep my vi - sions to ____ my - self.

It's on - ly me ___ who wants ___ to wrap a - round ___ your dreams. _

7

And have you an-y dreams you'd like to sell? ___ Dreams of lone-

-li-ness ___ like a heart-beat, drives you mad, ___ in the still - ness of re-mem-

ber-ing ___ what you had ___ and what you lost ___

and what you had ___ and what you lost. ___

Chorus

Oh, thun-der on-ly hap - pens when it's rain - ing.

Play - ers on-ly love ___ you when they're play - ing. ___

Say, wom-en, they will come ___ and they will go. ___

When the rain ___ wash-es ___ you clean, you'll know. _

Outro

You'll know. ___ You will know. ___ Oh, _

___ you'll know. ___

③ I Just Called to Say I Love You

Words and Music by Stevie Wonder

true,   made up of these three words ___ that I ___

Chorus

___ must say ___ to you: ___   I just called ___

___ to say ___   I love ___ you. ___

I just called ___   to say ___ how much ___ I care. ___

___ I just called ___   to say ___

___ I love _____ you. ___   And I mean ___

___ it from ___ the bot - tom of ___ my ___ heart.

Verse

3. No sum - mer's high;   no warm Ju -

ly;   no har - vest moon to light ___ one ten -

- der Aug - ust night. ___   No au - tumn

breeze; _____ no fal - ling leaves.

Not e - ven time for birds ___ to fly _____ to south - ern skies. _

___ 4. No Li - bra sun;

no Hal - low - een; no giv - ing

thanks to all _____ the Christ - mas joy _____ you bring. _____

But what it is, _____ though old so

new to fill your heart like no _____ three words _

Chorus

_____ could ev - er do: _____ I just called _

_____ to say _____ I love _____ you. _____

I just called _____ to say _____ how much ___ I care _

I just called _____ to say _____ I love _____ you. _____ And I mean _____ it from _____ the bot - tom of _____ my _____ heart. I just called _____ to say _____ I love _____ you. _____ I just called _____ to say _____ how much _____ I care. _____ I just called _____ to say _____ I love _____ you. _____ And I mean _____ it from _____ the bot - tom of _____ my _____ heart.

Outro

heart. Of my heart, of my

heart. _____

◆4 Let It Be

Words and Music by John Lennon and Paul McCartney

be. _____ For though they may _____ be part-

ed, there is still a chance that we'll _____ see. _____

There will be an an - swer: Let it be. _____

Chorus

Let it be, _____ let it be. _____ Let it be, _____

_____ let it be. _____ There will be an an - swer let it

be. _____ Let it be, let it be. Let it be, _____

_____ let it be. _____ Whis - per words _ of wis - dom: let it

Interlude

be. _____

3. And

Verse

when the night _ is cloud - y, there is still a light that shines _

5 (You Make Me Feel Like) A Natural Woman

Words and Music by Gerry Goffin, Carole King and Jerry Wexler

Verse

Moderately ♩ = 111

1. Look-in' out on the morn-ing rain, I used to feel un-in-spired. And when I knew I'd have to face an-oth-er day. Lord, it made me feel so tired. Be-fore the day I met you, life was so un-kind. Your love was the key to my peace of mind. 'Cause

Chorus

you make me feel, you make me feel, you make me feel like a nat-u-ral wom-an.

Verse

2. When my soul was in the lost and found, you came a-long to claim it.

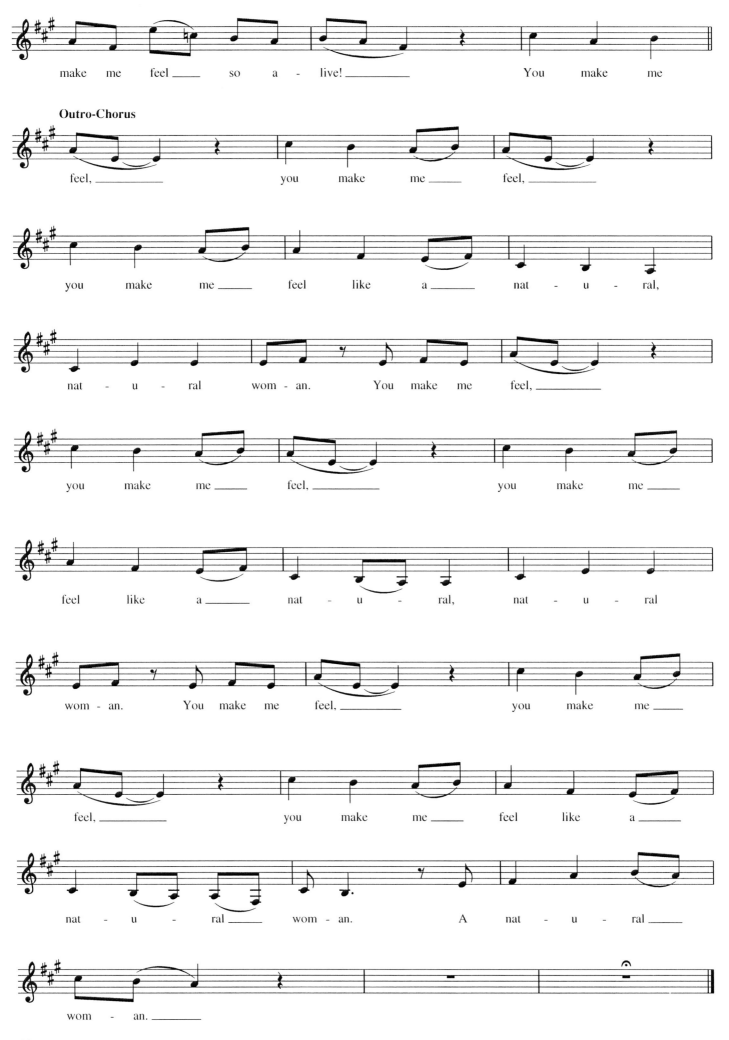

make me feel ____ so a - live! _____ You make me

Outro-Chorus

feel, _____ you make me ____ feel, _____

you make me ____ feel like a _____ nat - u - ral,

nat - u - ral wom - an. You make me feel, _____

you make me ____ feel, _____ you make me ____

feel like a _____ nat - u - ral, nat - u - ral

wom - an. You make me feel, _____ you make me ____

feel, _____ you make me ____ feel like a _____

nat - u - ral ____ wom - an. A nat - u - ral ____

wom - an. _____

Piece of My Heart

Words and Music by Jerry Ragovoy and Bert Berns

come ___ on,   come ___ on,   come ___ on,

Chorus

come ___ on and take it.   Take an - oth - er lit - tle piece of my heart,

___ now, ba - by, ___ oh, ___ break it!   Break an -

oth - er lit - tle bit off my heart, ___ now, dar - lin', yeah. ___ Yeah. Yeah. Yeah. _

Have a...   have an - oth - er lit - tle piece of my heart, ___ now, ba - by. _

Well, you know you got ___ it   if it

makes you feel good, ___ oh, yes in - deed. _

2. You're

Verse

out   on the streets ___ look - in' good.   And

deep down in your heart ___ I guess ya know it ain't right.

Well, you know you got ____ it if it makes you feel good, ___

Guitar Solo

___ oh, yes in - deed. ___

Pre-Chorus

I need you to come _____ on, come _____ on,

Chorus

come _____ on, come _____ on and take it. Take an -

oth - er lit - tle piece of my heart _____ now, ba - by. _____

7 Surfin' U.S.A.

Words and Music by Chuck Berry

at Wal - a - me - a Bay. _____ Ev - 'ry - bod - y's gone

surf - in', _____ surf - in' U. S. A. _____

Keyboard Solo

Guitar Solo

Ev - 'ry - bod - y's gone

Outro-Chorus

surf - in', _____ surf - in' U. S. A. _____

Ev - 'ry - bod - y's gone surf - in', _____ surf - in' U. S. A. _____

_____ Ev - 'ry - bod - y's gone surf - in', _____

surf - in' U. S. A. _____

Wonderful Tonight

Words and Music by Eric Clapton

Bridge

I feel won - der - ful ___ be - cause I see ___ the love ___ light in ___ your eyes. ___

___ And the won - der of it all ___ is that you just don't ___ re - al - ize ___

___ how much ___ I love ___ you.

Verse

3. It's time to go home ___ now. ___ I've got an ach - ing

head. I give her the car ___ keys, ___ and she helps me to

bed. And then I tell ___ her, ___

as I turn out the light, ___ I say, "My dar - lin', you are

won - der - ful ___ to - night." ___ Oh, my

Outro

dar - lin', you are won - der - ful ___ to - night. ___

28

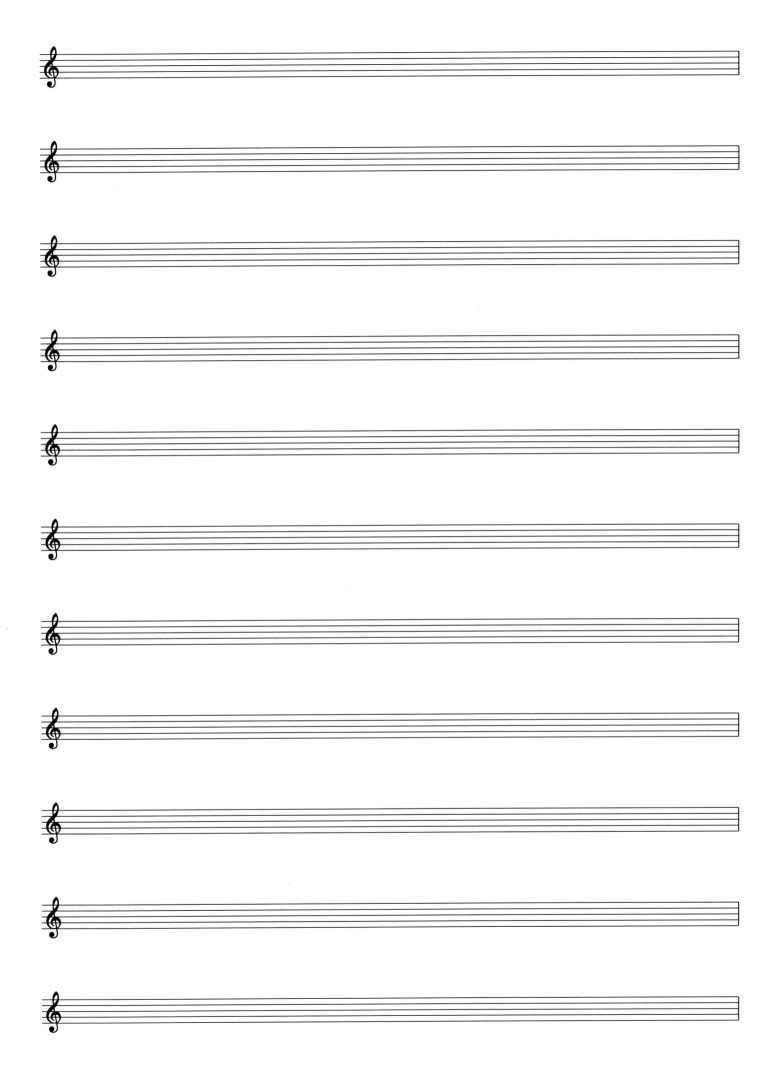

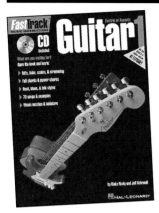

FastTrack® MUSIC INSTRUCTION

FastTrack is the fastest way for beginners to learn to play the instrument they just bought. **Fast**Track is different from other method books: we've made our book/CD packs user-friendly with plenty of cool songs that make it easy and fun for players to teach themselves. Plus, the last section of the **Fast**Track books have the same songs so that students can form a band and jam together. Songbooks for Guitar, Bass, Keyboard and Drums are all compatible, and feature eight songs including hits such as Wild Thing • Twist and Shout • Layla • Born to Be Wild • and more! All packs include a great play-along CD with a professional-sounding back-up band.

FASTTRACK GUITAR

For Electric or Acoustic Guitar – or both!
by Blake Neely & Jeff Schroedl
Book/CD Packs

Teaches music notation, tablature, full chords and power chords, riffs, licks, scales, and rock and blues styles. Method Book 1 includes 73 songs and examples.

LEVEL 1
00697282	Method Book – 9" x 12"	$7.99
00695390	Method Book – 5½" x 5"	$7.95
00697287	Songbook 1 – 9" x 12"	$12.95
00695397	Songbook 1 – 5½" x 5"	$9.95
00695343	Songbook 2	$12.95
00696438	Rock Songbook 1	$12.99
00696057	DVD	$7.99

LEVEL 2
00697286	Method Book	$9.99
00697296	Songbook 1	$12.95
00695344	Songbook 2	$12.95

CHORDS & SCALES
00697291	9" x 12"	$9.95
00696588	Spanish Edition	$9.99

FASTTRACK BASS

by Blake Neely & Jeff Schroedl
Book/CD Packs

Everything you need to know about playing the bass, including music notation, tablature, riffs, licks, scales, syncopation, and rock and blues styles. Method Book 1 includes 75 songs and examples.

LEVEL 1
00697284	Method Book – 9" x 12"	$7.95
00697289	Songbook 1 – 9" x 12"	$12.95
00695400	Songbook 1 – 5½" x 5"	$9.95
00695368	Songbook 2	$12.95
00696440	Rock Songbook 1	$12.99
00696058	DVD	$7.99

LEVEL 2
00697294	Method Book	$9.95
00697298	Songbook 1	$12.95
00695369	Songbook 2	$12.95

FASTTRACK KEYBOARD

For Electric Keyboard, Synthesizer, or Piano
by Blake Neely & Gary Meisner
Book/CD Packs

Learn how to play that piano today! With this book you'll learn music notation, chords, riffs, licks, scales, syncopation, and rock and blues styles. Method Book 1 includes over 87 songs and examples.

LEVEL 1
00697283	Method Book – 9" x 12"	$7.99
00697288	Songbook 1 – 9" x 12"	$12.95
00695366	Songbook 2	$12.95
00696439	Rock Songbook 1	$12.99
00696060	DVD	$7.99

LEVEL 2
00697293	Method Book	$9.95
00697297	Songbook 1	$12.95
00695370	Songbook 2	$12.99

CHORDS & SCALES
00697292	9" x 12"	$9.95

FASTTRACK DRUM

by Blake Neely & Rick Mattingly
Book/CD Packs

With this book, you'll learn music notation, riffs and licks, syncopation, rock, blues and funk styles, and improvisation. Method Book 1 includes over 75 songs and examples.

LEVEL 1
00697285	Method Book – 9" x 12"	$7.95
00695396	Method Book – 5½" x 5"	$7.95
00697290	Songbook 1 – 9" x 12"	$12.95
00695367	Songbook 2	$12.95
00696441	Rock Songbook 1	$12.99

LEVEL 2
00697295	Method Book	$9.95
00697299	Songbook 1	$12.95
00695371	Songbook 2	$12.95
00696059	DVD	$7.99

FASTTRACK SAXOPHONE

by Blake Neely
Book/CD Packs

With this book, you'll learn music notation; riffs, scales, keys; syncopation; rock and blues styles; and more. Includes 72 songs and examples.

LEVEL 1
00695241	Method Book	$7.95
00695409	Songbook	$12.95

FASTTRACK HARMONICA

by Blake Neely & Doug Downing
Book/CD Packs

These books cover all you need to learn C Diatonic harmonica, including: music notation • singles notes and chords • riffs, licks & scales • syncopation • rock and blues styles. Method Book 1 includes over 70 songs and examples.

LEVEL 1
00695407	Method Book	$7.99
00695574	Songbook	$12.95

LEVEL 2
00695889	Method Book	$9.95

FASTTRACK LEAD SINGER

by Blake Neely
Book/CD Packs

Everything you need to be a great singer, including: how to read music, microphone tips, warm-up exercises, ear training, syncopation, and more. Method Book 1 includes 80 songs and examples.

LEVEL 1
00695408	Method Book	$7.99
00695410	Songbook	$12.95
00696589	Spanish Edition	$7.99

LEVEL 2
00695892	Songbook 1	$12.95

FOR MORE INFORMATION, SEE YOUR LOCAL MUSIC DEALER, OR WRITE TO:

HAL•LEONARD® CORPORATION
7777 W. BLUEMOUND RD. P.O. BOX 13819 MILWAUKEE, WI 53213

Visit Hal Leonard online at **www.halleonard.com**

Prices, contents, and availability subject to change without notice. Some products may not be available outside the U.S.A.

1211